Seasons of the
Tundra Biome

Written by
Shirley Duke

Rourke
Educational Media

rourkeeducationalmedia.com

Scan for Related Titles
and Teacher Resources

www.rourkeeducationalmedia.com

PHOTO CREDITS: Cover photo © sasha384; Title page © Incredible Arctic; page 4 © Matthew Jacques; map © Christian Lopetz; notebook © PixelEmbargo; page 5 © Iakov Filimonov, pages 6 and 7 © Pi-Lens; page 8 © outdoorsman; page 9 © Sergey Uryadnikov; page 10 © Ryan DeBerardinis, page 10 inset photo © Thomas W. Woodruff; page 11 © Walter Quirtmair; page 12 © Okhotnikova Ekaterina; page 13 © Vladimir Melnik; page 14 © by Alla; page 15 © Knumina Studios; page 16 © visceralimage; page 16 inset photo © Howard Sandler;page 17 © Jeff McGraw; page 18 © Maslov Dmitry; page 19 © Pim Leijen; page 20 © Smileus; page 21 © atbaker

Edited by Jill Sherman

Cover design by Renee Brady
Interior design by Nicola Stratford bdpublishing.com

Library of Congress PCN Data

Seasons of the Tundra Biome / Shirley Duke
(Biomes)
ISBN 978-1-62169-897-5 (hard cover)
ISBN 978-1-62169-792-3 (soft cover)
ISBN 978-1-62717-004-8 (e-Book)
Library of Congress Control Number: 2013936813

Also Available as:
ROURKE'S
e-Books

Rourke Educational Media
Printed in the United States of America,
North Mankato, Minnesota

Rourke
Educational Media

rourkeeducationalmedia.com

customerservice@rourkeeducationalmedia.com • PO Box 643328 Vero Beach, Florida 32964

Table of Contents

Windy and Cold

Everywhere you look you see wide, open land. There are no trees. You feel the cold wind blowing and you shiver. Where are you? The **tundra.**

Most Tundras have:
- ✓ Long, dark winter days.
- ✓ Long, bright summer days.
- ✓ Very cold temperatures year-round.
- ✓ Little snow or rain.
- ✓ Underground ice that never thaws.
- ✓ Flat landforms.

Tundra

Ice stays just under the soil year-round. It does not **thaw**.

Tundra is found in the northern parts of the world. Alaska, Canada, and parts of Russia are tundra. The tundra may look bare and cold to you, but it is home to many animals and plants.

The Snowy Owl is covered head-to-toe with thick feathers, which protect it from severe winter weather.

Changing Seasons

When does it get really cold in the tundra? Fall brings the first **freeze**.

If you visit the tundra in fall, a rainbow of colors greets you. Plants turn red, yellow, and orange.

Tundra plants grow close together. This helps hold their short roots in the ground in high winds.

Then, in winter, deep cold sinks in to stay.

Would you like to live in the dark? In the tundra, winter darkness lasts 24 hours a day.

32°F / 0°C

-94°F / -70°C

Freezing Point

Lowest Recorded
Tundra Temperature

Tundra is the coldest of all the biomes.

Arctic foxes, wolves, and polar bears have thick fat and fur, which protect them from the cold.

The polar bear's small ears cut down heat loss.

The short spring is a very active time. Birds return. They are busy building nests. Animal babies are born.

Whistling swans stay in flocks except when breeding.

Caribou

Many young tundra animals can walk soon after birth. They must be able to run to escape their predators.

During the short summer, the Sun never sets! The warm summer sunshine melts the ice. The water **pools** to make **bogs** and ponds.

Summer sunshine melts the ice on top of the soil. The water sinks in and then stops. The ice under the soil keeps it from going deeper.

The tundra summer lasts just six to eight weeks.

If you look closely you will find moss, **lichens**, and short grass covering the ground in summer. Can you see the wildflowers that dot the carpet of plants?

Adapting to Life

How do animals survive on the tundra year-round? Small, busy creatures live on the tundra. **Hares**, squirrels, and **voles** eat grasses and short plants like mosses and lichens. So do reindeer. But the small creatures must watch out for predators like foxes and wolves.

Arctic ground squirrels eat grasses, mushrooms, willows, roots, stalks, leaves, flowers, and seeds.

Birds are predators too. Snow buntings and ruddy turnstones dine on thick clouds of insects at the bogs.

The Gyrfalcon is the largest falcon species with a wingspan reaching up to 64 inches (164 centimeters).

Did you know that some animals change colors? Arctic foxes and Arctic hares have brown fur in summer. Then their fur turns white in winter.

Arctic fox

Arctic hare

Why do the animals change colors? They need to blend in with the land so they can hide from predators.

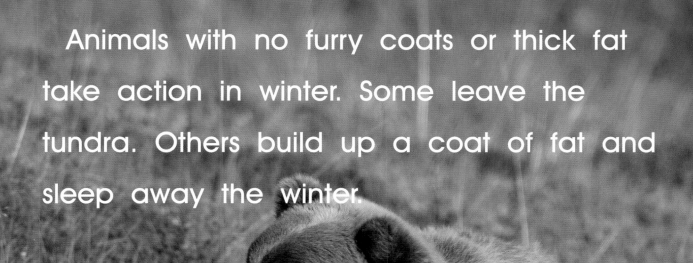

Animals with no furry coats or thick fat take action in winter. Some leave the tundra. Others build up a coat of fat and sleep away the winter.

Brown bears gain weight by eating berries, fruits, and other food in the fall. Then, they retire to dens, where they stay until spring.

Future of the Tundra

Even small changes hurt tundra life. The warming Earth is the big problem.

Warm air is melting the ice under the soil. People hurt the land with drilling and pollution.

Air pollution kills lichens, a source of food for many animals.

The tundra holds food for many creatures.
Any change can keep plants from growing.
This hurts all life on the tundra.

The red fox moved north in search of food. It now roams where the Arctic fox lives. They must fight for the same food.

You can help the tundra. Use power from green sources to reduce pollution.

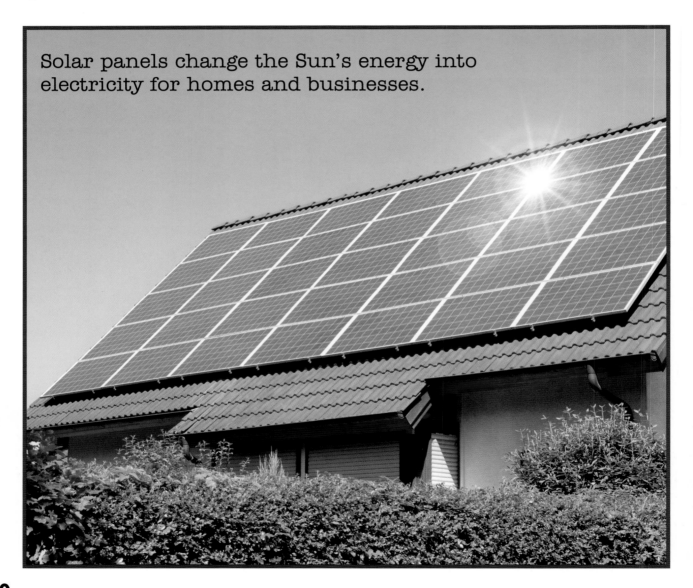

Solar panels change the Sun's energy into electricity for homes and businesses.

The tundra is a beautiful and unique place. Let's work together to protect the tundra.

National parks preserve the natural beauty of the land. They also protect wildlife and the environment from being harmed.

You Can Help Protect the Tundra:

✓ Reduce air pollution.
✓ Reduce oil use.
✓ Don't drill on the tundra.
✓ Protect the land with parks.
✓ Teach people about why we need the tundra.

Study Like a Scientist
Looking at Lichens

1. Find a lichen.

2. Remove the lichen.

3. With care, pull it apart.

4. Look at the two plants.

Which part do you think makes the food?

If you guessed the green part, you were right!

Glossary

bogs (BAHGZ): sections of wet, soft land

freeze (FREEZ): when water becomes solid at a cold temperature

hares (HAIRZ): mammals like rabbits but with larger ears and stronger back legs

lichens (LYE-kuhns): flat, gray-green plants formed of two plants that grow on rocks, trees, and walls

pools (POOLZ): collects and comes together

thaw (THAW): to melt

tundra (TUHN-druh): a biome in the north with no trees and a layer of frozen soil underground

voles (VOLZ): small mammals in the rat family that tunnel under the snow

Index

Websites

www.enchantedlearning.com/biomes/tundra/tundra.shtml

www.kids.nceas.ucsb.edu/biomes/tundra.html#games

animal.discovery.com/guides/mammals/habitat/map.html

About the Author

Shirley Duke has enjoyed learning science all of her life and she's written many books about it. She lives in Texas and New Mexico and enjoys the different seasons in each place. Her favorite thing to do is visit places she's read and written about. One day she hopes to visit the tundra, in the summer!

Meet The Author!
www.meetREMauthors.com